The Inspiring Business Lessons of Amancio Ortega Gaona:

Unlocking the Secrets to Fashion Industry Success and Wealth Creation.

By

Vincenzo D. Hill

This publication's content is fully protected by copyright law. Reproduction, distribution, or transmission in any form or by any means, including photocopying, recording, or any electronic or mechanical methods, is strictly prohibited without prior written permission from the publisher. Short quotes may be used in reviews or for certain noncommercial purposes permitted by copyright law. Any unauthorized use or reproduction violates the copyright holder's rights.

Copyright © Vincenzo D. Hill, 2024.

Table of Contents

Introduction.. 4

Chapter 1: The Early Years........................... 13

Chapter 2: Starting a Business...................... 22

Chapter 3: The Rise of Zara..........................32

Chapter 4: Fast Fashion Revolution............. 42

Chapter 5: Learning from Customers.......... 52

Chapter 6: Smart Supply Chain Management 63

Chapter 7: The Role of Technology.............. 75

Chapter 8: Building a Strong Brand.............88

Chapter 9: Leadership and Teamwork.......100

Chapter 10: Lessons for Future Entrepreneurs... 109

Conclusion.. 119

Introduction

Understanding Amancio Ortega: The Man Behind Zara

Amancio Ortega is a very important person in the fashion world. He was born on March 28, 1936, in a small town in Spain called Busdongo de Arbas. Growing up, he did not have a lot of money. His family was not rich, but they worked hard. Ortega learned to appreciate the value of money and hard work from an early age.

When he was young, Ortega started working at a local shop. He delivered shirts to customers. This job taught him how clothing was made and sold. He learned how to take care of customers and what they liked. He also worked in a tailor's shop, where he saw how clothes were made. These experiences helped him understand the fashion business very well.

In 1963, Ortega opened his first company, Confecciones Goa, which made bathrobes. He noticed that many clothing companies were using expensive materials, which made clothes cost more. Ortega wanted to make clothes that were stylish and affordable. He thought about how to make clothes that people wanted to wear but at lower prices. This was the beginning of his journey into the world of fashion.

In 1975, Ortega opened the first Zara store in A Coruña, Spain. Zara quickly became popular because it offered trendy clothes at reasonable prices. Ortega believed in creating new styles quickly. He used ideas from fashion shows and made clothes that people wanted to buy right away. This fast production cycle helped Zara grow rapidly.

Ortega's way of doing business is called "fast fashion." This means creating clothes quickly and getting them into stores as soon as possible. While other brands took months to design and produce clothes, Zara was able to do it in just a few weeks. This quick turnaround made Zara special and very successful.

Why His Lessons Matter in Business

Amancio Ortega's story teaches us many valuable lessons about business. First, he shows us the importance of understanding the market. He listened to customers and watched what was happening in the fashion world. Ortega paid attention to trends and what people wanted to wear. By understanding the market, he was able to create clothes that appealed to many customers. This lesson reminds us that knowing our customers is very important in any business.

Another important lesson from Ortega is to be innovative. He was always looking for new ways to improve his business. For example, he used technology to make production faster and better. Zara's use of technology in design and supply chain management is a big reason for its success. Ortega's willingness to embrace new ideas shows us that innovation can lead to growth and success.

Amancio Ortega also teaches us about the value of hard work. Despite his success, he has always been known for being humble and working hard. He did not seek the spotlight and preferred to keep a low profile. This attitude is important because it shows that success comes from dedication and effort, not just fame or fortune. Ortega's life encourages us to focus on our work and goals instead of seeking attention.

Teamwork is another key lesson from Ortega's story. He built a strong team at Inditex, which is the company behind Zara. He knew that having a good team was essential for success. By working together, they were able to come up with great ideas and keep the business running smoothly. This shows that collaboration and communication are crucial for any business.

Furthermore, Ortega teaches us the importance of adaptability. The fashion industry is always changing, and businesses must change with it. Ortega was quick to change Zara's designs based on customer feedback and current trends. This ability to adapt to market demands helped Zara remain relevant and popular. In business, being flexible and willing to change is vital for long-term success.

Sustainability is also becoming a significant topic in the fashion industry today. While Ortega's fast fashion model is popular, it also raises questions about the environment. Many people are now looking for brands that care about sustainability. This shift teaches us that businesses need to consider their impact on the world. Learning to balance success with responsibility is essential for future entrepreneurs.

Lastly, Ortega's journey emphasizes the importance of having a clear vision. He always knew what he wanted to achieve and worked hard to reach his goals. His focus on creating stylish, affordable clothes made

Zara a global brand. Having a vision helps guide decisions and keep businesses on the right track.

In summary, Amancio Ortega is not just a successful businessman; he is a source of inspiration for many people. His life story shows us that anyone can achieve great things with hard work, creativity, and a willingness to learn. The lessons from his journey are valuable for anyone interested in business. They remind us to understand our customers, innovate, work hard, build strong teams, adapt to changes, consider sustainability, and have a clear vision.

As we explore the business lessons of Amancio Ortega, we will learn how his approach to fashion can apply to various industries. His strategies can inspire future entrepreneurs to think creatively and work diligently toward their goals. By following in his footsteps, anyone can unlock the secrets to success and wealth creation in their own lives.

Chapter 1: The Early Years

Growing Up in Spain

Amancio Ortega was born on March 28, 1936, in a small village in Spain called Busdongo de Arbas. This village is located in the northwestern part of the country. Ortega was born into a simple family. His father worked as a railway worker, and his mother stayed at home to take care of the family. They did not have a lot of money, but they valued hard work and education.

Ortega was the youngest of four children. His family moved to A Coruña when he was just a boy. A Coruña is a big city near the ocean. The city had many shops, markets, and beautiful streets. Growing up in this city helped Ortega learn about business and customers. He watched how people bought things and what they liked to wear.

In A Coruña, Ortega had to adapt to a new life. He attended school and made friends. However, when he was just 14 years old, he left school to help his family. He wanted to contribute to their income and learn how to make a living. This decision showed his strong work ethic and determination to succeed.

First Jobs: Learning the Trade

After leaving school, Ortega started working in a small shop that sold shirts. His job was to deliver the shirts to customers. He rode a bicycle around the city, carrying the shirts in a big bag. While he delivered the shirts, he learned how to talk to customers and understand their needs. This experience taught him the importance of good service and how to make people happy.

Later, Ortega worked as an assistant in a tailor's shop. There, he saw how clothes were made from start to finish. He learned about fabrics, styles, and designs. The tailor taught him how to measure people and make clothes that fit well. Ortega loved this job. He became fascinated with fashion and how clothing could change the way people looked and felt.

While working at the tailor's shop, Ortega started to think about his own ideas. He wanted to create clothes that were beautiful but also affordable. He noticed that many people wanted stylish clothes, but they could not always afford them. This observation was important because it planted the seeds for his future success.

Ortega's early jobs gave him valuable lessons. He learned about hard work, dedication, and the importance of customer satisfaction. He realized that understanding what people want is key to success in business. These experiences helped him develop a strong foundation for his future in the fashion industry.

Discovering the Fashion World

As Ortega continued working, he became more interested in the fashion world. He noticed that styles changed often, and new trends appeared every season. He started to visit fashion shows and read fashion magazines. He wanted to understand what was popular and what people wanted to wear.

During the late 1950s, Ortega began to see the potential in the fashion industry. He understood that people wanted to wear clothes that made them feel good. He also saw that many fashion brands focused on expensive materials and complicated designs. Ortega believed he could create a different kind of fashion—one that was stylish, affordable, and accessible to everyone.

In 1963, Ortega decided to start his own business. He founded a company called Confecciones Goa, which made bathrobes. He chose to create bathrobes because they were simple and comfortable. He used materials that were less expensive but still looked nice. This approach allowed him to sell his products at lower prices. People loved his bathrobes because they were both stylish and affordable.

The success of Confecciones Goa encouraged Ortega to think bigger. He realized that if he could sell bathrobes, he could also sell other types of clothing. He wanted to create a brand that offered a wide range of stylish clothes at prices that everyone could afford. This idea was the beginning of his journey into the fashion industry.

Ortega's discovery of the fashion world was not just about creating clothes; it was about understanding people. He learned how to listen to customers and identify their needs. He also saw how important it was to adapt to changing trends. Fashion is always evolving, and Ortega wanted to be part of that change.

His early experiences in the fashion world prepared him for the challenges ahead. Ortega was determined to succeed and willing to work hard to make his dreams come true. He learned that success in business requires not just talent, but also perseverance, creativity, and a deep understanding of customers.

Ortega's journey in the fashion industry began with small steps. From delivering shirts to creating his own bathrobe business, he built a strong foundation. Each job and experience contributed to his knowledge and skills. These lessons would help him as he moved forward in the fashion world.

Conclusion of Chapter 1

In this chapter, we explored the early years of Amancio Ortega's life. He grew up in a humble family in Spain and learned the value of hard work from an early age. His first jobs in the clothing business taught him important lessons about customer service and the fashion industry. By discovering his passion for fashion, Ortega set the stage for his future success.

Ortega's experiences shaped him into a determined entrepreneur. He understood the needs of his customers and was ready to create a brand that would change the fashion industry. As we continue to learn about Ortega's journey, we will see how these early years influenced his decisions and helped him build a global fashion empire.

Chapter 2: Starting a Business

The Birth of Confecciones Goa

In 1963, Amancio Ortega took a big step. He decided to start his own company called Confecciones Goa. He was excited but also a little nervous. Ortega wanted to make clothes that people would love, but he knew that starting a business was not easy.

Ortega began by focusing on bathrobes. He thought bathrobes were a smart choice because they were simple to make and people used them every day. Many people liked to wear bathrobes at home. They were comfortable and warm. Ortega believed he could create beautiful bathrobes that were also affordable.

To start his business, Ortega needed a few important things. First, he needed a place to work. He found a small workshop in A Coruña, where he had grown up. This workshop had enough space for him to make bathrobes and store the materials. He bought fabric and other supplies to begin making his products.

Ortega worked hard in the workshop. He designed the bathrobes himself and oversaw the production. He chose soft and nice-looking fabrics that people would enjoy wearing. He also made sure that the bathrobes were well-made, so they would last a long time.

At first, Ortega did not have many workers. He relied on a few friends and family members to help him. They all worked together to create the first batch of bathrobes. Each person had a role, and teamwork was essential. Ortega motivated his team with his passion and enthusiasm.

Soon, Ortega finished making the first bathrobes. They were ready to be sold. Ortega knew that he needed to find customers. He decided to sell his bathrobes at local markets and shops. He wanted to reach people who cared about quality and style.

Making Bathrobes: A Smart Start

Making bathrobes was a smart start for Ortega's business. He understood that people wanted comfortable clothes they could wear at home. By focusing on bathrobes, he created a product that was in demand. Ortega paid close attention to details while making the bathrobes. He wanted them to be perfect.

Ortega learned how to choose the right fabrics. He looked for materials that were soft and durable. He wanted people to feel comfortable and relaxed when they wore his bathrobes. He also experimented with different colors and styles. This way, he could offer a variety of options to his customers.

Ortega's hard work paid off. People started to notice his bathrobes. They loved the quality and design. The word spread quickly. Customers began to tell their friends and family about the bathrobes. This word-of-mouth marketing helped Ortega attract more buyers.

As sales increased, Ortega realized he needed to grow his business. He expanded his workshop and hired more workers. With a bigger team, he could produce more bathrobes in less time. This allowed him to meet the growing demand.

Ortega also started to think about how to make his bathrobes even better. He wanted to create styles that were trendy and appealing. He watched fashion shows and kept an eye on what was popular. This helped him stay updated on the latest trends. He understood that fashion was always changing, and he wanted his business to adapt.

Understanding Costs and Profits

One of the most important lessons Ortega learned was understanding costs and profits. He knew that to succeed, he needed to keep track of how much money he spent to make his bathrobes. He carefully calculated the costs of materials, labor, and other expenses.

Ortega learned that if he wanted to make money, he had to sell the bathrobes for a higher price than what it cost to make them.

This is called profit. He aimed for a fair price that customers would be willing to pay. At the same time, he wanted to ensure he could cover his costs and still make a profit.

Ortega kept detailed records of his expenses. He noted how much he spent on fabric, thread, and even the electricity to run the workshop. By keeping track of everything, he could see where he could save money. This helped him make smart decisions.

For example, Ortega found that buying fabric in bulk was cheaper than buying small amounts. This allowed him to lower his costs and increase his profits. He used this strategy to keep his prices competitive while still providing quality products.

He also learned about customer preferences. If a certain style of bathrobe was popular, he produced more of that style. This helped him sell more and earn more money. Understanding what customers wanted allowed him to make better decisions for his business.

As Confecciones Goa grew, Ortega became more focused on managing the business. He spent time studying the market and learning about other successful companies. He wanted to understand what made them thrive. He attended trade shows and talked to other business owners. This helped him gain valuable insights and ideas.

Ortega also understood the importance of customer feedback. He listened to what people said about his bathrobes. If customers wanted a different color or style, he made changes. This flexibility helped him create products that met customer needs and preferences.

Conclusion of Chapter 2

In this chapter, we learned about Amancio Ortega's journey in starting his business, Confecciones Goa. He made smart choices by focusing on bathrobes, understanding costs, and learning about customer preferences. His hard work, attention to detail, and ability to adapt helped him build a successful company.

Ortega's experiences taught him important lessons about running a business. He learned how to make quality products, manage expenses, and listen to customers. These skills would serve him well as he continued to grow and develop in the fashion industry.

As we move forward, we will see how these early successes set the stage for Ortega's future accomplishments. His commitment to quality and understanding of business would play a vital role in his later ventures, including the creation of Zara and Inditex.

Chapter 3: The Rise of Zara

Opening the First Zara Store

In 1975, Amancio Ortega took a big step forward. He opened the first Zara store in A Coruña, Spain. This was not just any store; it was a place where people could find stylish and affordable clothes. Ortega wanted Zara to be different from other clothing shops. He aimed to create a shopping experience that made people feel excited.

The store was designed to look modern and inviting. The windows displayed beautiful outfits that caught the eye of passersby. Inside, the store had a clean and organized layout. Customers could easily find what they were looking for. Ortega knew that the look and feel of the store were important for attracting shoppers.

Zara offered a variety of clothes for men, women, and children. The selection included trendy outfits, classic styles, and accessories. Ortega wanted to ensure that everyone could find something they liked. He believed that fashion should be accessible to all. This made Zara a popular choice for many people.

The first Zara store was a success. Customers loved the clothes and the shopping atmosphere. They appreciated the high quality at affordable prices. The store quickly gained a loyal following. People began to visit Zara regularly, eager to see the new styles and designs.

Ortega's approach to fashion was different from other retailers. He focused on creating new styles quickly, inspired by the latest trends. While other stores took months to develop new clothing lines, Zara could design, produce, and sell items in just a few weeks. This quick turnaround kept the inventory fresh and exciting.

What Made Zara Special?

Zara became special for several reasons. First, it offered stylish clothes at prices that most people could afford. Many shoppers found it difficult to pay high prices for fashionable clothing. Zara solved this problem by providing good quality at lower prices. People felt happy to buy trendy clothes without spending a lot of money.

Another factor that made Zara unique was its ability to quickly respond to fashion trends. Ortega and his team carefully studied what was happening in the fashion world. They looked at runway shows, street fashion, and customer feedback. By staying aware of trends, Zara could design clothes that customers wanted almost immediately.

Zara's success also came from its limited inventory. Instead of producing a large number of each item, Zara made only a few pieces. This strategy created a sense of urgency among shoppers. When people saw something they liked, they felt they had to buy it quickly. If they waited too long, it might be gone. This helped Zara sell out of items faster and made customers eager to return for new arrivals.

The store layout and shopping experience were also important. Zara aimed to create a friendly environment. The stores were bright, and the staff was helpful. Customers felt welcome and comfortable while shopping. This positive experience encouraged them to come back again and again.

Ortega also focused on keeping costs low. He managed production efficiently and worked closely with manufacturers. This allowed Zara to offer fashionable clothes without high expenses. By keeping costs in check, Zara could pass the savings onto customers.

The Power of Location and Design

Location played a significant role in Zara's success. Ortega understood that having stores in the right places was essential. He chose busy areas with lots of foot traffic. These locations attracted more customers and helped Zara grow its brand.

In cities, Zara often set up shop on main streets or in popular shopping districts. These high-traffic areas ensured that many people would see the store. Ortega believed that visibility was crucial for drawing in customers. The more people who saw Zara, the more potential buyers it had.

The design of the stores also contributed to Zara's appeal. Each store was carefully arranged to highlight the clothing. The bright lighting showcased the colors and details of the garments. This made everything look attractive and inviting. The layout allowed customers to explore the collections easily.

Zara also changed its displays frequently. Every few weeks, the store would refresh the layout and feature new clothing. This made it exciting for customers to visit, as they would see something different each time. It created a sense of anticipation, encouraging them to come back regularly to see what was new.

Ortega also valued simplicity in design. The clothing was displayed neatly and organized by style. This made it easy for customers to browse and find what they liked. The clean and modern aesthetic matched the clothing, enhancing the overall shopping experience.

The combination of location, design, and customer-focused strategies helped Zara rise in popularity. People began to associate Zara with trendy, affordable fashion. It became a go-to place for shoppers looking for stylish clothing.

Conclusion of Chapter 3

In this chapter, we explored the rise of Zara and how it became a successful fashion brand. Amancio Ortega opened the first

Zara store in 1975, creating a unique shopping experience. Zara stood out because it offered stylish clothes at affordable prices and quickly adapted to fashion trends.

The store's design and location played a vital role in attracting customers. Zara became known for its friendly atmosphere and well-organized layout. Ortega's focus on quality, cost control, and customer preferences contributed to the brand's growth.

As Zara continued to expand, it set new standards in the fashion industry. Ortega's vision and dedication led to the creation of a brand that would change the way people shopped for clothes. In the next chapter, we will look at how Zara grew beyond Spain and became an international fashion leader.

Chapter 4: Fast Fashion Revolution

What is Fast Fashion?

Fast fashion is a way of making and selling clothes that is quick and affordable. It allows people to buy trendy clothing without spending too much money. The term "fast fashion" refers to the speed at which fashion moves from the runway to the stores. It focuses on creating styles that are inspired by high fashion but at a much lower price.

In the past, fashion changes took a long time. Designers would create new styles for the seasons, and it could take months for those designs to reach stores. With fast fashion, this process has become much faster. Brands like Zara can design, produce, and sell new clothing in just a few weeks. This means customers can buy the latest styles almost right after they see them on models or celebrities.

Fast fashion is also about offering a wide variety of choices. Customers can find many different styles, colors, and sizes in one store. This makes shopping exciting because there is always something new to discover. People can find clothes for any occasion, whether it's for work, a party, or everyday wear.

Another important aspect of fast fashion is the idea of keeping prices low. Fast fashion brands use efficient production methods to keep costs down. This way, they can offer trendy clothes at prices that everyone can afford. Many people appreciate being able to wear stylish outfits without breaking the bank.

However, fast fashion does have some drawbacks. The quick production methods can sometimes lead to lower quality clothing. Many fast fashion items are not made to last. They may fall apart after a few washes or become outdated quickly. This can create waste because people often throw away clothes that are no longer in style or that they no longer want.

How Zara Stays Ahead of Trends

Zara has a special way of staying ahead of fashion trends. The brand keeps a close eye on what is happening in the fashion world. They pay attention to runway shows, fashion blogs, and social media to see what styles are popular. By staying updated, Zara can create clothes that people want to buy.

One of the keys to Zara's success is its strong team of designers and buyers. These professionals work together to analyze trends and develop new styles. They take inspiration from various sources, including street fashion and cultural events. This means that Zara can quickly respond to what customers are looking for.

Zara also uses customer feedback to guide its designs. The brand listens to what shoppers say about the clothing. If customers love a certain style, Zara can produce more of it. If something is not selling well, they can change the design or replace it with something new. This flexibility helps Zara keep its inventory fresh and appealing.

Another way Zara stays ahead is through its efficient supply chain. The company has strong relationships with manufacturers, which allows them to produce clothing quickly. When a new design is ready, it can be made and sent to stores in just a few weeks. This quick turnaround ensures that customers always find new items when they visit Zara.

Zara also creates limited quantities of each style. This creates a sense of urgency among shoppers. When people see that only a few pieces are available, they feel they must buy quickly before it sells out. This strategy keeps customers coming back to see what new styles have arrived. It also helps Zara maintain its reputation for being trendy and current.

Making Fashion Quickly and Efficiently

Zara's ability to make fashion quickly and efficiently is one of its most significant advantages. The brand has developed a unique system that allows it to produce clothing faster than traditional retailers. This system is known as "just-in-time" production.

In just-in-time production, Zara only makes what it needs based on current demand. This means that instead of producing large quantities of clothing that may not sell, Zara creates smaller batches. This reduces waste and allows for quicker adjustments based on customer preferences.

Zara also focuses on local production. While many companies produce clothing overseas, Zara often works with manufacturers closer to its home base in Spain. This allows for faster shipping and quicker restocking of popular items. If a style is selling well, Zara can quickly make more and get them to stores within days.

Technology plays a significant role in Zara's efficiency. The company uses advanced software to track inventory and sales. This information helps Zara understand which items are popular and which are not. By using data to inform its decisions, Zara can avoid overproducing and ensure that it always has the right items in stock.

Zara also emphasizes teamwork and communication. The design, production, and retail teams work closely together. This collaboration ensures that everyone is on the same page. When a new design is approved, it can go into production right away, reducing delays.

The combination of just-in-time production, local manufacturing, advanced technology, and teamwork allows Zara to create fashionable clothing quickly and efficiently.

This approach has made Zara a leader in the fast fashion industry.

Conclusion of Chapter 4

In this chapter, we learned about the fast fashion revolution and how it has changed the clothing industry. Fast fashion offers quick and affordable clothing options for customers. Zara stands out in this field by staying ahead of trends and responding quickly to customer needs.

Zara's efficient production methods, limited inventory, and strong team have helped it become a leader in fast fashion. By focusing on what customers want and making changes quickly, Zara keeps its clothing fresh and exciting.

As we move on to the next chapter, we will explore Zara's expansion into international markets and how it became a global fashion powerhouse.

Chapter 5: Learning from Customers

Listening to Shoppers: A Key Strategy

Zara knows that its success comes from listening to its customers. The brand understands that shoppers are the heart of its business. When people buy clothes, they want to feel happy and satisfied with their choices. Zara has developed a smart strategy to listen carefully to what shoppers say and want.

One way Zara listens to customers is through feedback. When someone buys a piece of clothing, they may talk about it with friends or share their thoughts online. Zara pays attention to these conversations. The company uses surveys and social media to gather opinions about its clothes. This information helps the brand understand what people like and dislike.

Zara also has a team of store employees who interact with customers every day. These employees hear what shoppers say while they browse the store. They can observe which items customers try on and which ones they buy. This firsthand information is valuable because it gives Zara insights into customer preferences.

Another important part of Zara's listening strategy is its quick response time. When customers express their thoughts about a specific item, Zara acts fast. If a certain style is very popular, Zara can make more of it quickly. If a piece of clothing does not sell well, the brand can remove it from the shelves and create something new. This agility allows Zara to stay connected to what customers want at all times.

Adapting Styles Based on Feedback

Listening to customers is just the first step. Zara takes it a step further by adapting its styles based on feedback. This means that if customers say they want a different color, size, or style, Zara can make those changes. This adaptability is a significant part of why Zara is successful.

For example, if a new dress is popular but shoppers want it in a different color, Zara can quickly adjust the design. Instead of waiting for the next season to release a new collection, Zara can produce the new color within weeks. This quick turnaround keeps customers excited and eager to shop.

Zara also listens to feedback about fit and comfort. If customers say a shirt is too tight or a pair of pants is uncomfortable, Zara takes note. The design team can then work on making improvements. By listening closely to shoppers, Zara creates clothing that not only looks good but also feels good.

Adapting styles based on feedback builds strong relationships with customers. Shoppers feel valued when a brand listens to their opinions. When people see that their feedback leads to changes, they are more likely to return to Zara. This loyalty is essential for the brand's long-term success.

Why Customer Satisfaction Matters

Customer satisfaction is a crucial element of Zara's strategy. When customers are happy, they tend to come back for more. Satisfied shoppers are more likely to recommend Zara to their friends and family. This word-of-mouth advertising is powerful and can bring new customers to the brand.

Zara focuses on providing an excellent shopping experience. This includes friendly customer service, a clean and organized store, and easy returns. When customers have a positive experience, they feel good about their purchases. They are more likely to leave the store with a smile and a desire to return.

Zara also knows that satisfied customers are more likely to share their experiences online. In today's world, many people look at reviews and ratings before making a purchase. If Zara receives positive feedback, it can attract new customers who are curious about the brand. On the other hand, if customers are unhappy, it can harm Zara's reputation. This is why customer satisfaction is so important.

The brand regularly conducts customer satisfaction surveys to measure how well it is doing. These surveys ask shoppers about their experiences in-store and online. The feedback helps Zara identify areas for improvement. Whether it's adding new styles or improving customer service, Zara uses this information to keep customers happy.

Building a Customer-Centric Culture

Zara has built a customer-centric culture. This means that every part of the business focuses on meeting customer needs. From design to production and sales, Zara's teams work together to ensure that shoppers are happy. Everyone at Zara knows that satisfied customers lead to success.

The design team collaborates with the marketing team to understand customer preferences. When creating new styles, they keep customer feedback in mind. This teamwork ensures that Zara creates clothing that people want to buy. It also helps the brand stay relevant in a fast-changing industry.

Training is another essential part of Zara's customer-centric culture. Employees are taught how to interact with customers and listen to their needs. They learn to ask questions and understand what shoppers are looking for. This training helps create a positive shopping environment where customers feel welcome and appreciated.

Zara also values diversity among its employees. By having a team with different backgrounds and perspectives, the brand can better understand its customers. This diversity allows Zara to create clothing that appeals to a wide range of people.

The Impact of Customer Engagement

Engaging with customers has a significant impact on Zara's success. When customers feel connected to the brand, they are more likely to become loyal shoppers. Zara encourages customer engagement through social media and online platforms. Shoppers can share their thoughts and experiences with the brand and connect with other fans.

Zara actively participates in conversations on social media. The brand responds to comments, answers questions, and shares new styles. This interaction helps build a community around the brand, making customers feel like they are part of something special.

Additionally, Zara uses customer engagement to launch marketing campaigns. The brand often showcases customer photos and feedback in its advertising. This approach creates a sense of belonging and makes customers feel valued. When shoppers see their friends wearing Zara clothes, they are more likely to consider buying from the brand.

Conclusion of Chapter 5

In this chapter, we learned about the importance of learning from customers. Zara's strategy of listening to shoppers helps the brand adapt its styles based on feedback.

This adaptability is crucial for maintaining customer satisfaction.

By focusing on what customers want, Zara creates a strong connection with its shoppers. Satisfied customers return, spread the word, and help the brand grow. In the next chapter, we will explore Zara's global expansion and how it became a leading name in fashion around the world.

Chapter 6: Smart Supply Chain Management

Understanding Supply Chains

A supply chain is like a long path that clothes take from the factory to the store. It starts with raw materials and ends with customers buying clothes. Zara's supply chain is very smart. This means the brand can make clothes quickly and keep costs low. Let's break down what a supply chain is and why it matters.

In a supply chain, many people and companies work together. Some grow cotton for fabric, while others sew clothes. Each step in the chain is important. If one step is slow or has problems, it can affect the whole process. Zara understands that to be successful, it must have a smooth supply chain. This way, the brand can provide customers with the latest fashion at affordable prices.

Zara's supply chain is unique because it can respond quickly to changes in fashion. When a new trend appears, Zara can get new clothes to the stores in just a few weeks. This is much faster than many other brands. Most companies take months to release new styles. Zara's ability to move quickly is a big reason for its success.

Keeping Production Close to Home

One of the key strategies Zara uses is keeping production close to home. Most of Zara's factories are in Europe, especially in Spain and Portugal. This is different from many other clothing brands that produce their items far away, in countries like China or Bangladesh.

By keeping factories nearby, Zara can quickly create new clothes. If a design needs changes, the company can make adjustments fast. This is important because fashion trends can change in the blink of an eye. When customers want something new, Zara can respond immediately.

Another advantage of nearby production is quality control. Zara can monitor the quality of the clothes better when factories are close. This means customers get well-made items that they love. If a shirt has a small problem, Zara can fix it quickly. This focus on quality helps build trust with customers.

Keeping production close also helps reduce shipping times. When Zara needs to send clothes to stores, it takes less time if the factories are nearby. This means customers can find new styles on the shelves sooner. They do not have to wait long for the latest fashion trends.

Reducing Costs and Increasing Speed

Zara's smart supply chain also helps the brand reduce costs. By producing clothing close to home, the company saves money on shipping and transportation. When items are made in nearby factories, there is less distance to travel. This leads to lower shipping fees, which means more savings for Zara.

Zara also produces smaller batches of clothing. This is different from many brands that make a lot of one style. When Zara creates fewer items, it can test how well they sell. If a style is popular, Zara can quickly make more. If it is not popular, Zara can stop making it. This way, the brand reduces waste and only produces what customers want.

Smaller production runs also mean that Zara can change styles often. New designs can hit the stores faster. Customers love having new choices. This quick turn-around keeps them coming back for more.

Another way Zara reduces costs is by using technology. The company uses special software to manage its supply chain. This software helps Zara track how much clothing is made, where it is located, and when it needs to be shipped. By using technology, Zara can make better decisions and keep costs low.

Zara also has a team of experts who focus on supply chain management. These professionals ensure everything runs smoothly. They plan how to get materials, how to make clothes, and how to ship them. This careful planning is key to keeping costs down and speed high.

The Role of Data in Supply Chain Management

Data plays a big role in Zara's supply chain. The company collects information about what styles customers like and how often they buy them. This data helps Zara know what to produce and how much to make.

For example, if Zara sees that a specific shirt is selling quickly, it can decide to make more of that shirt. If another style is not selling, it can reduce production. This data-driven approach helps Zara make smart decisions that save money and time.

Zara also uses data to predict trends. The company looks at what people are wearing and what is popular in the market. This information helps Zara create new styles that customers will love. By staying ahead of trends, Zara can keep its stores filled with clothes that shoppers want.

Collaborating with Suppliers

Another important part of Zara's supply chain is its strong relationships with suppliers. The brand works closely with fabric and material suppliers to ensure quality and speed. When Zara needs materials, it can quickly get what it needs because of these good relationships.

Zara also collaborates with suppliers to create new materials. This innovation helps the brand stand out. For example, if Zara wants a unique fabric for a new style, it can work with suppliers to develop it. This cooperation leads to better products and keeps Zara at the forefront of fashion.

Strong supplier relationships also help reduce risks. If a supplier has a problem, Zara can quickly find another source. This flexibility ensures that production continues smoothly without interruptions. It also means that Zara can deliver new styles to stores without delays.

The Impact of Supply Chain on Sustainability

Zara is becoming more aware of its impact on the environment. The brand understands that a smart supply chain can also support sustainability. By producing clothing close to home, Zara reduces the carbon footprint from transportation. This is good for the planet.

Zara also focuses on using sustainable materials. The company works with suppliers to find eco-friendly fabrics. By using materials that are better for the environment, Zara shows its commitment to sustainability. This is important for customers who care about where their clothes come from.

Zara has set goals to reduce waste in its supply chain. The brand wants to ensure that clothes are made responsibly. This includes using less water and energy during production. By adopting sustainable practices, Zara can help protect the environment while still delivering fashion to its customers.

Conclusion of Chapter 6

In this chapter, we learned how Zara uses smart supply chain management to succeed in the fashion industry. Understanding supply chains helps the brand stay ahead of trends and keep costs low. By producing clothing close to home and using technology, Zara can quickly respond to customer needs.

Zara's focus on data, collaboration with suppliers, and sustainability are also important factors in its success. These strategies help the brand maintain quality while providing customers with the latest fashion at affordable prices. In the next chapter, we will explore Zara's marketing strategies and how they attract customers worldwide.

Chapter 7: The Role of Technology

Using Technology in Fashion

Technology has changed the way we create, sell, and buy clothes. In the fashion world, using technology helps brands like Zara stay successful. Zara uses advanced tools and methods to design clothes, manage its stores, and understand customers better. This is important for staying ahead in a competitive market.

One of the main ways technology helps Zara is in design. Designers use computer software to create clothing patterns. This software makes it easy to change colors, shapes, and sizes quickly. When designers have an idea, they can see it on the screen right away. This saves time and helps create better clothes.

Another way technology is used is through 3D printing. This means making a product using a machine that builds it layer by layer. Zara can create samples of new clothes quickly with 3D printing. Instead of waiting for fabric to arrive, designers can see and touch their ideas much faster. This helps them make decisions and changes quickly.

Technology also helps Zara manage its inventory. Inventory is the number of clothes in the store or warehouse. Zara uses special software to track what clothes are available. This way, when a shirt is selling well, Zara knows to make more. If a style is not popular, they can stop making it. This keeps stores full of items that customers want.

Online Shopping: A New Era

The internet has changed how people shop for clothes. Zara has embraced this change by offering online shopping. This means customers can buy clothes from anywhere with just a few clicks. They do not need to go to the store. This makes shopping easy and convenient.

Zara's website is designed to be user-friendly. It is simple to navigate, and customers can find what they want quickly. They can browse different categories, like men's, women's, or children's clothing. Customers can see pictures of the clothes, read descriptions, and check sizes without leaving their homes.

Online shopping also allows Zara to reach more customers around the world. People in different countries can shop on the same website. This helps Zara grow its customer base. The company can sell more clothes and become more popular globally.

Zara also uses technology to enhance the online shopping experience. For example, customers can see what clothes look like on different models. This helps them imagine how the clothes might look on themselves. Zara also offers a "virtual fitting room" where customers can see how items fit without trying them on.

Another important feature is easy returns. If a customer does not like what they ordered, they can send it back. Zara provides clear instructions on how to return items. This makes shopping online less stressful, encouraging more customers to buy.

Data-Driven Decisions for Success

Data is information that helps businesses make smart choices. Zara collects a lot of data to understand its customers better. This data includes what clothes customers buy, when they buy them, and what styles they like. By analyzing this information, Zara can make better decisions.

For example, if Zara sees that a particular dress is popular, it can produce more of that style. If a certain color is selling well, they can create more clothes in that color. This data helps Zara know what customers want, ensuring the stores always have what shoppers are looking for.

Zara also uses data to track customer behavior. This means understanding how customers interact with the website and the stores. For example, if many customers visit a specific page on the website but do not buy anything, Zara can investigate why. They can then make changes to improve the shopping experience.

Another way data helps Zara is by managing trends. Fashion trends can change quickly, and data allows Zara to keep up. By looking at what customers are wearing and what is popular on social media, Zara can adapt its designs. This keeps the brand relevant and in line with what people want to wear.

Zara also collects feedback from customers. This feedback can come from reviews, surveys, and social media comments. Listening to what customers say helps Zara understand their likes and dislikes. If customers suggest changes, Zara can consider them when designing new clothes. This feedback loop keeps customers happy and engaged.

The Importance of Speed

In the fashion industry, speed is crucial. Zara uses technology to ensure its supply chain is fast. This means getting new clothes from the design stage to the store quickly. When trends change, Zara can respond almost immediately.

Using technology allows Zara to streamline its processes. For example, computer software helps manage orders, inventory, and production schedules. This efficiency reduces delays and ensures that new styles are available as soon as possible. When customers see new clothes in stores, they feel excited and eager to buy.

Zara's quick turnaround time is a significant advantage over many competitors. Other brands might take months to launch new styles. In contrast, Zara can get new designs to stores in a few weeks. This speed helps Zara remain a favorite among shoppers who want the latest fashions.

Enhancing Customer Experience

Technology also helps improve the overall customer experience. Zara uses apps and online tools to connect with customers. Customers can easily browse the latest collections and even get alerts when new items arrive. This keeps them informed and excited about shopping.

Zara also uses technology in its physical stores. For example, some stores have interactive screens where customers can browse styles, check sizes, and even find items in stock. This technology enhances the shopping experience by making it easier for customers to find what they need.

Additionally, Zara offers personalized recommendations based on past purchases. If a customer frequently buys casual wear, Zara can suggest similar styles. This personalized approach makes shopping more enjoyable and helps customers find clothes they love.

Sustainability and Technology

Zara is becoming more focused on sustainability, and technology plays a vital role in this effort. By using data to track materials and production processes, Zara can make smarter choices. For example, if a fabric is not environmentally friendly, Zara can look for better alternatives.

Technology helps Zara reduce waste in its supply chain. By tracking inventory and sales data, Zara can produce only what is needed. This means fewer unsold items go to waste. This is an essential step toward becoming a more sustainable brand.

Zara also uses technology to inform customers about sustainable practices.

Through its website and apps, customers can learn about the brand's efforts to be eco-friendly. This transparency builds trust and encourages customers to support the brand.

Conclusion of Chapter 7

In this chapter, we explored how technology plays a crucial role in Zara's success. From design to online shopping and data-driven decisions, technology helps Zara stay ahead in the fashion industry. The ability to respond quickly to trends and understand customer preferences allows Zara to provide the latest styles.

Zara's commitment to using technology enhances the shopping experience for customers. As technology continues to advance, Zara will likely find new ways to innovate and improve. In the next chapter, we will look at Zara's marketing strategies and how they attract customers worldwide.

Chapter 8: Building a Strong Brand

What Makes Zara a Strong Brand?

Zara is one of the most recognized fashion brands in the world. But what makes Zara so strong? There are several reasons for its success. First, Zara is known for its trendy clothes. People see Zara as a brand that always has the latest styles. This reputation keeps customers coming back for more.

Another reason Zara is strong is its ability to change quickly. Unlike other brands that take months to create new styles, Zara can bring new designs to stores in just a few weeks. This speed is impressive and makes customers excited to shop. When they know they can find something new every time they visit, they are more likely to return.

Zara also offers a variety of clothing for everyone. From casual wear to formal outfits, there is something for everyone at Zara. This wide range attracts many customers. Families can shop together and find clothes that fit their needs.

Additionally, Zara is known for its quality. While the prices are affordable, the clothes are well-made. Customers appreciate this balance of quality and price. They feel they are getting good value for their money. This satisfaction helps build a loyal customer base.

The Importance of Consistency

Consistency is key to building a strong brand. Zara understands this very well. From the way they design clothes to how they present themselves in stores, Zara maintains a consistent look and feel. This consistency helps customers recognize the brand immediately.

For example, Zara uses a simple and clean store layout. The clothes are displayed neatly, making it easy for customers to browse. The lighting in the stores is bright, and the overall atmosphere is inviting. This environment makes shopping enjoyable and encourages customers to explore.

Zara also keeps a consistent style in its marketing materials. Whether it's an online ad or a poster in the store, the visuals are always similar. The color schemes and fonts are the same, creating a cohesive brand image. This helps people remember Zara and associate it with fashion.

Moreover, Zara is consistent in its communication. The brand interacts with customers on social media and through emails. They respond quickly to questions and feedback. This approach builds trust. Customers know they can rely on Zara for good service.

Being consistent does not mean Zara is boring. Instead, it allows the brand to stay relevant. By consistently delivering quality and style, Zara keeps customers engaged. People feel they know what to expect when they shop at Zara.

Marketing Strategies without Heavy Advertising

Zara is unique because it does not rely on heavy advertising like many other brands. Instead, it uses smart marketing strategies to promote itself. One of the main ways Zara does this is through word-of-mouth. When customers love a product, they talk about it. They share their experiences with friends and family. This creates a buzz around the brand without spending a lot on ads.

Zara also relies on its store locations to attract customers. Many Zara stores are in popular shopping areas. People naturally walk by these stores while shopping. Bright displays and trendy window designs catch their attention. This draws in customers who may not have planned to shop at Zara.

Another effective strategy is creating limited editions of certain styles. By offering unique pieces that are only available for a short time, Zara encourages customers to buy quickly. They don't want to miss out on something special. This sense of urgency can lead to increased sales.

Zara also pays attention to customer feedback. By listening to what customers want, Zara can adapt its styles accordingly. This responsiveness shows customers that their opinions matter. It also helps Zara create clothes that people want to buy, making the brand more popular.

The Role of Social Media

Social media plays a big part in Zara's marketing strategy. The brand uses platforms like Instagram and Facebook to connect with customers. Zara shares images of new collections, styling tips, and fashion trends. These posts keep customers engaged and excited about the brand.

Zara encourages customers to share their looks on social media. When customers post photos of themselves wearing Zara clothes, it acts as free advertising. Other people see these posts and may want to shop at Zara too. This organic promotion is powerful.

Zara also collaborates with influencers. Influencers are people with many followers on social media. When they wear Zara clothing and share it online, their followers take notice. This kind of marketing reaches new audiences and helps Zara gain more customers.

Sustainable Practices as a Marketing Tool

Zara is becoming more focused on sustainability, and this is part of its brand strategy. Many customers today care about the environment. They want to support brands that share their values. Zara promotes its efforts to be more eco-friendly, such as using sustainable materials and reducing waste.

By sharing information about these practices, Zara builds a positive image. Customers appreciate knowing that their favorite brand cares about the planet. This commitment to sustainability can attract new customers and keep current ones loyal.

Zara also runs campaigns to raise awareness about sustainability. They educate customers on how to take care of their clothes to make them last longer. This message resonates with many people who want to make more conscious shopping choices.

Building Relationships with Customers

Zara focuses on building strong relationships with its customers. This strategy is crucial for maintaining a strong brand. By understanding their customers' preferences, Zara can create a shopping experience that feels personal. Customers feel valued when a brand listens to their needs.

Zara collects data on customer preferences and buying habits. This information helps them tailor their marketing efforts. For example, if a customer frequently buys casual wear, Zara can send personalized recommendations. This shows customers that Zara pays attention to what they like.

The company also engages customers through loyalty programs. These programs reward customers for shopping at Zara. By offering discounts or exclusive access to new collections, Zara encourages customers to return. This builds loyalty and strengthens the brand.

Conclusion of Chapter 8

In this chapter, we learned what makes Zara a strong brand. Its trendy designs, quick response to trends, and commitment to quality attract customers. Consistency in branding and smart marketing strategies help Zara stand out in a crowded market.

Zara's use of social media, sustainable practices, and customer relationships further enhance its brand strength. By focusing on what customers want and need, Zara can create a shopping experience that keeps people coming back.

In the next chapter, we will explore Zara's international expansion and how it became a global fashion powerhouse.

Chapter 9: Leadership and Teamwork

Ortega's Leadership Style

Amancio Ortega, the founder of Zara, is known for his unique leadership style. He is not a typical boss who sits in an office all day. Instead, Ortega believes in being involved in all aspects of the business. He often walks through the stores and production areas to see how everything works. This hands-on approach helps him understand what customers want and how the team can do better.

Ortega is also a quiet leader. He does not like to be in the spotlight. Instead of giving big speeches, he leads by example. His work ethic inspires others. He shows that dedication and hard work can lead to success. People in the company admire him for this. They see how much he cares about the brand and its customers.

His leadership style encourages everyone to be involved. Ortega believes that every employee has valuable ideas. He listens to them and values their opinions. This makes employees feel important and respected. When they know their voices matter, they are more likely to work hard and contribute to the team.

Ortega's leadership is also focused on teamwork. He believes that success comes from working together. He encourages collaboration among different departments. This means designers, marketers, and store managers communicate well. When everyone works as a team, they can create better products and experiences for customers.

Building a Great Team

Building a great team is essential for any successful business, and Zara is no different. Ortega focuses on hiring the right people. He looks for individuals who are passionate about fashion and dedicated to their work. These qualities help create a team that shares the same goals and vision.

Zara also values diversity in its team. People from different backgrounds bring different perspectives. This variety helps the company create clothing that appeals to a wide range of customers. A diverse team can understand the needs of various groups, which is important for a global brand like Zara.

Training is another important aspect of building a great team. Zara invests in training programs to help employees develop their skills. From design to customer service, training ensures that everyone knows their role. When employees feel confident in their abilities, they perform better.

Zara also promotes a positive work environment. Employees are encouraged to share ideas and collaborate. This open atmosphere allows team members to learn from each other. They can discuss new designs or marketing strategies together. This teamwork leads to more creative solutions.

When employees are happy at work, they are more productive. They enjoy coming to work and feel motivated to do their best. A strong team spirit helps everyone feel connected. This unity makes Zara a great place to work.

Encouraging Innovation and Creativity

Zara thrives on innovation and creativity. Ortega understands that the fashion industry changes quickly. To stay ahead, Zara needs fresh ideas and unique designs.

He encourages employees to think outside the box. Creativity is vital for keeping the brand relevant.

One way Zara fosters innovation is through regular brainstorming sessions. Employees from different departments come together to share their ideas. This collaboration can lead to exciting new designs or marketing campaigns. Everyone's input is valued, creating a sense of ownership over the brand's success.

Zara also allows employees to experiment. Designers can try new styles and materials without strict guidelines. This freedom leads to innovative products that customers may love. When employees feel free to be creative, they often produce exceptional work.

Feedback is an important part of the creative process at Zara. After a new design is launched, the team gathers information on customer reactions. They look at sales data and listen to customer feedback. This information helps them understand what works and what doesn't. When employees see their ideas making a difference, it motivates them to keep innovating.

Technology also plays a role in encouraging creativity at Zara. The company uses advanced tools to help designers visualize their ideas. This technology makes it easier to create and test new designs. When designers can quickly see their concepts come to life, it sparks their imagination.

Conclusion of Chapter 9

In this chapter, we explored the importance of leadership and teamwork in Zara's success. Amancio Ortega's unique leadership style inspires dedication and hard work. His focus on collaboration helps create a strong team that is passionate about the brand.

Building a great team requires hiring the right people, promoting diversity, and providing training. A positive work environment encourages employees to share ideas and work together. This teamwork leads to better products and a stronger brand.

Finally, Zara's commitment to innovation and creativity keeps it ahead of trends. By encouraging brainstorming, allowing experimentation, and utilizing technology, Zara fosters a culture of creativity. This culture helps the brand stay fresh and exciting for customers.

In the next chapter, we will look at how Zara successfully expanded into international markets and became a global leader in fashion.

Chapter 10: Lessons for Future Entrepreneurs

Key Takeaways from Ortega's Journey

Amancio Ortega's journey with Zara offers valuable lessons for future entrepreneurs. First, he shows that hard work is very important. Ortega started with little money and built a successful company. He worked long hours and was dedicated to his dream. This determination helped him succeed. It teaches future business owners that they need to put in effort and not give up easily.

Second, Ortega emphasizes the importance of understanding your market. He paid close attention to what customers wanted. By listening to shoppers and responding to their needs, he created products that sold well. Entrepreneurs should learn to know their customers. Understanding what people like helps in creating products they want to buy.

Another key lesson is the value of teamwork. Ortega built a strong team at Zara. He encouraged collaboration and valued everyone's ideas. This teamwork led to creativity and better products. Entrepreneurs should remember that they cannot do everything alone. Having a supportive team makes a big difference in achieving goals.

Lastly, Ortega's journey teaches us about flexibility. The fashion world changes quickly. Ortega adapted to new trends and customer feedback. This flexibility helped Zara stay successful. Future entrepreneurs should be open to change. They should learn to adjust their strategies when needed to keep up with their market.

Tips for Success in Business

Here are some practical tips for success in business inspired by Ortega's story:

1. Work Hard: Success does not come overnight. Put in the time and effort to reach your goals. Be prepared to work long hours and stay focused.

2. Know Your Customers: Listen to what your customers say. Understand their needs

and preferences. This information helps you create products they will love.

3. Build a Strong Team: Surround yourself with people who share your vision. Hire individuals who are skilled and passionate. Encourage teamwork and value everyone's input.

4. Stay Organized: Keep track of your goals, tasks, and finances. Organization helps you manage your business more effectively. It also allows you to focus on important tasks without feeling overwhelmed.

5. Be Flexible: The business world can change quickly. Be ready to adapt your plans. Listen to feedback and make changes

when necessary. This adaptability will keep your business relevant.

6. Keep Learning: Always seek knowledge. Read books, attend workshops, and learn from others in your field. Staying informed helps you make better decisions.

7. Use Technology: Embrace technology to improve your business. It can help you streamline processes, reach customers, and analyze data effectively.

8. Set Clear Goals: Define what you want to achieve. Setting specific and measurable goals keeps you focused. Break your goals into smaller steps to make them easier to reach.

9. Market Wisely: Use marketing strategies that suit your target audience. You do not need to spend a lot on advertising. Use social media and word of mouth to spread the word about your brand.

10. Stay Positive: Keep a positive attitude, even when facing challenges. A positive mindset helps you overcome obstacles and motivates your team.

Staying True to Your Vision

A vital lesson from Ortega's journey is the importance of staying true to your vision. Every entrepreneur has a unique idea or goal that drives them. It is essential to keep that vision in mind as you build your business.

Ortega had a clear vision for Zara. He wanted to create fashionable clothing that was affordable for everyone. This vision guided all his decisions. It helped him stay focused during tough times. Future entrepreneurs should also define their vision clearly. Writing it down can help solidify it in their minds.

Staying true to your vision also means being authentic. Do not try to copy others just because they are successful. Find your own path and make your business unique. This authenticity attracts customers who appreciate what you stand for.

Sometimes, challenges may arise that test your vision. There may be temptations to compromise your values for quick profits.

However, sticking to your vision builds trust with your customers. When people see that you are genuine, they are more likely to support your brand.

Additionally, your vision can evolve over time. As you grow and learn, you may discover new aspects of your passion. It is okay to adapt your vision while still staying true to your core values. This growth shows that you are learning and improving.

To help stay connected to your vision, regularly reflect on your goals. Ask yourself if your actions align with your vision. If not, make adjustments to get back on track. This reflection keeps your business aligned with your purpose.

Conclusion of Chapter 10

In this chapter, we explored valuable lessons for future entrepreneurs from Amancio Ortega's journey. Key takeaways include the importance of hard work, understanding customers, building a strong team, and being flexible. These lessons can guide new business owners in their journey.

We also discussed practical tips for success, such as staying organized, using technology, and setting clear goals. Each of these tips can help entrepreneurs navigate the challenges of starting and running a business.

Finally, we highlighted the significance of staying true to your vision. A clear vision guides decisions and keeps you focused on your goals. It is essential to be authentic and true to your values as you grow your business. By following these lessons, future entrepreneurs can increase their chances of success while building brands that they believe in.

Conclusion

Recap of Amancio Ortega's Impact

Amancio Ortega is a name that many people know because he built Zara, one of the most successful clothing brands in the world. His journey began in Spain, where he started with little money. Ortega worked very hard, and his efforts paid off. He created a fashion empire that changed the way people shop for clothes.

Zara is known for its unique way of doing business. It introduced the idea of "fast fashion." This means that Zara can design, produce, and sell new clothes very quickly. While other brands take months to release new styles, Zara can do it in just a few weeks. This speed keeps customers excited and coming back for more.

Ortega also focused on understanding what customers wanted. He listened to their feedback and made changes to his products based on what shoppers liked. This connection with customers helped Zara become a favorite brand for many people. It showed that businesses should pay attention to their customers to succeed.

Another important aspect of Ortega's impact is how he created a strong brand. Zara is recognized around the world for its stylish and affordable clothing. The brand is consistent in its quality and design, which builds trust with customers. When people see Zara, they know they will find trendy clothes at reasonable prices.

Ortega's leadership style played a crucial role in Zara's success. He built a strong team and encouraged them to be creative. This teamwork led to innovative ideas and unique clothing designs. Ortega showed that a successful business relies on the people working in it. By valuing his team, he created a positive work environment that fosters creativity.

Final Thoughts on Success and Wealth Creation

Amancio Ortega's story teaches us valuable lessons about success and wealth creation. Success is not just about making money; it is about creating something meaningful. Ortega started with a vision and worked tirelessly to turn it into reality. His journey shows that hard work, determination, and a clear goal can lead to great achievements.

Wealth creation is not only about profits; it is also about making a positive impact. Ortega's approach to business has inspired many other companies to focus on what customers want. This customer-centric mindset has transformed the retail industry. It shows that businesses can be successful while also caring about their customers and their needs.

Moreover, Ortega's story highlights the importance of adaptability. The business world changes quickly, and being flexible is key. Ortega adapted to new trends and technologies, which helped Zara stay ahead of competitors. This lesson is crucial for anyone looking to succeed in business. Being open to change can lead to new opportunities and growth.

Another significant takeaway is that success can come from anywhere. Ortega started from humble beginnings but built a global brand. His story proves that with dedication and the right mindset, anyone can achieve their dreams. It encourages aspiring entrepreneurs to believe in themselves and take risks.

Inspiring the Next Generation of Business Leaders

Amancio Ortega's journey serves as an inspiration for the next generation of business leaders. Young people can learn from his example to build their own successful businesses. They should remember that hard work, creativity, and a strong vision can lead to great things.

Future entrepreneurs can look at Ortega's ability to listen to customers. Understanding what people want is a critical part of building a business. Young leaders should engage with their customers and learn from their feedback. This connection can help them create products that people will love.

Another lesson for young leaders is the importance of teamwork. Ortega valued his employees and created a supportive work environment. Future entrepreneurs should surround themselves with a strong team that shares their vision. Encouraging collaboration and creativity among team members can lead to innovative ideas and success.

Additionally, young business leaders should embrace technology. Ortega used technology to improve Zara's operations and reach customers. Future entrepreneurs should explore how technology can enhance their businesses. Whether through online sales, social media, or data analysis, technology can provide valuable tools for growth.

Finally, aspiring business leaders should stay true to their vision. Ortega had a clear idea of what he wanted to achieve. This focus helped him navigate challenges and stay on track. Young entrepreneurs should define their goals and remain committed to them, even when faced with obstacles.

In conclusion, Amancio Ortega's impact on the fashion industry and business as a whole is immense. His journey from humble beginnings to building a global brand teaches valuable lessons about hard work, customer connection, teamwork, and adaptability. As we look to the future, Ortega's story will inspire many young leaders to pursue their dreams and create successful, meaningful businesses. By learning from his example, the next generation can build a brighter future and contribute positively to the world.